RECIPE FOR RECOVERY

Group Process for Women's Addictions to Violence, Self-Destruction, and Abuse

Mary Blomgren

Learning Publications, Inc.
Holmes Beach, Florida

ISBN 1-55691-164-5

© 1999 by Mary Blomgren

All rights reserved. No part of this book may be reproduced or transmitted in any form or by any means, electronic or mechanical, including photocopying and recording, or by any information or retrieval systems, without permission in writing from the publisher.

Learning Publications, Inc.
5351 Gulf Drive
P.O. Box 1338
Holmes Beach, FL 34218-1338

Printing: 5 4 3 2 1   Year: 3 2 1 0 9

Book design by Belle Vista Graphics

Printed in the United States of America

Dedication

*To my husband and children
for understanding and supporting
my need to work and write.*

Contents

- 1   Attention Gourmets: Foreword
- 7   The 4A's Recipe: Setting Up A Group
    - 9   Using the Posters and Handouts
    - 10   Group Guidelines
- 11   Basic Tools: Discussions and Handouts
    - 13   Affirmations
    - 15   Behavior Change
- 17   Preparation: The Checklists
    - 20   Self-Esteem
    - 21   Parenting
    - 22   Self-Destruction
    - 23   Self-Affirmation
- 25   Mixing, Stirring, Blending and Folding: Discussions and Handouts
    - 27   Attitude Adjustment
    - 30   Basic Alanon
    - 32   Family System
    - 34   What Is My Business?
    - 36   Denial
    - 38   Codependency
    - 41   Feelings
    - 42   Awareness of Abuse
    - 44   Vocabulary
- 47   Baking and Cooling: Group Exercises
    - 49   Aftercare Planning
    - 52   Detachment
    - 55   Self-Esteem
- 57   Serving: Afterwords
    - 59   Closing Statement
    - 60   Basic Recipe for Recovery
    - 61   Pebbles and Popcorn
- 63   The Cookbook: Resources
    - 65   Counselor's Vocabulary
    - 67   Bibliography
    - 69   Internet
    - 71   Violence Wheel
    - 73   Non-Violence Wheel
    - 75   Order Form for Color Posters
    - 78   Black and White Pull-Out Posters

Acknowledgement

*To the staff and clients of
The A.W.A.R.E. Project for Women
in their willingness to share and grow.*

Special Mention

*To all the wonderful human beings
who share their recovery tools
on a daily basis.*

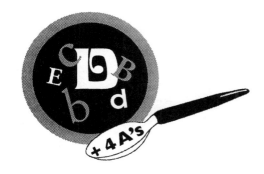

Attention Gourmets

FOREWORD

Foreword

Welcome to the **4A's,** stirred with patience, time, and skill:

Awareness of abuse and its many behaviors and feelings;

Acceptance of abuse and victim's part in abuse;

Action required changing abusive responses; and

Attitude required for short-term cooperation and long-term success.

As a Certified Addiction professional with 13 years in the field of Alcoholism and Addiction, I am writing this workbook with the full understanding of the dynamics of this field of work. We are counselors, nurses, psychologists and psychiatrists working to treat a cunning and baffling disease. Let us combine our strengths and support our weaknesses in this work.

Some of us agree to disagree on whether this is a disease or just self-will and self-indulgence. For this text I would ask we agree to disagree on what I have to say and what I suggest. Suggestion here is the key.

Addiction offers us the opportunity to work with people for short lengths of time and often repeated times, therefore experiential, "let's try this," can bring to your practice or clinic a breath of fresh air. There is information here we professionals could use to aid our own frustration with this "problem"/this disease. These are old ideas in new clothing.

The AMA and APA agree on six factors for diagnosis of this disease:

1. Primary illness exists in and of itself.
2. Chronic illness that is here to stay no matter what treatment.
3. Progressive physically no matter what happens psychologically.
4. Symptomatic in behavior and lifestyle leading to diagnosis.
5. Fatal if untreated.
6. Treatable starting with the removal of the poison.

I would suggest for the purpose of success in any treatment that the focus start with the removal of the poisonous substance and then work on the poisonous behaviors.

I would like us to agree on the significance of treating women separately.

Women face particularly difficult obstacles in removing alcohol and drugs from their lifestyle. As the caretakers of men and children, they face shame and guilt and secrecy issues.

Women work more effectively with the barriers of men and children removed. My experience from five years and two dissertations on women and children in an outpatient treatment center supports the effectiveness of separateness. The first dissertation is "Preventing Child Abuse through Teaching Positive Parenting Techniques." The second dissertation is "Identifying and Treating Self-Destructive Behaviors in Addicted Women through Group Process." Both research projects took place with the full support of a diverse staff offering individual support to the clients. All the exercises are tested and re-tested with mixed results. People who want recovery are successful. We need never forget how powerfully drugs and alcohol affect the lives of our clients.

In today's changing healthcare field, there are three strong selling points for group process:

1. It is less costly, using staff and time frugally.
2. It is a known safety factor for clients.
3. It allows levels of learning to occur (clients' shared experiences combined with staff skills).

Taking into consideration the **Set as a Drug Free Environment** and the **Setting as Group,** we can move forward into the meat of this workbook. My research shows that over a 12-week period women can become aware of their behavior, and with time and support from staff and clients, accept their self-destruction and, with luck, move into action to change. I offer the 4A's (awareness, acceptance, action, attitude adjustment) approach to treatment.

Those areas that stand out in my work are an addiction to people who abuse and use women.

The women are drawn to this verbal and physical abuse from their own lack of self-esteem and from a family history of similar behavior — a familiar dysfunction level passed from generation to generation. Separating women from these people, if only for three hours, gives some light to a dark place (guilt). Much time is spent in identifying abusive behaviors, separating what has been a lifelong norm into a package of choices for recovery.

Abuse is about control and it has a pattern — physical, emotional, sexual, economic, or a combination of behaviors used to control and keep control. We see this in repeated drug use, switching drugs from alcohol to cocaine to heroin and back to valium, combining drugs from speed-balling heroin/cocaine to smoking pot while drinking. What we need to talk about are abusive behaviors of partners:

Hit, grabbed, choked, bitten, burned, slapped, or pushed.

Used a gun or knife or some kind of weapon.

Hit you with some object — bat, pan, belt.

Hit, held, or squeezed you so hard that it left a bruise.

Threatened to hurt or kill you or your children or friends.

Withheld money or food or medicine or transportation.

Called you names, made you feel ashamed, humiliated you.

- Put you down in front of your children, friends, boss.
- Forced you to have sex when you did not want to.
- Forced you to perform sexual acts.
- Destroyed or broken your possessions, pets.
- Threatened to harm or kill himself/herself if you didn't do something.
- You felt like killing self rather than stay.
- You felt responsible for all of this.

Food is the next most obvious tool for self-destruction. Whether in starvation, bulimia, or over-eating, every woman has a pattern of acting out her low self-esteem by the misuse of food/fuel. This poor nutrition, physical and psychological abuse is passed on to those around the women, the children and spouses. Group discussion and a nutritionist when available are good solutions.

Third is the awareness of **Self-Care.** Teeth that need cleaning and filling, hair that needs washing and cutting, personal hygiene that needs new guidelines all are approached through group process. Dressing for successful recovery, dating tips, working a 12-step program and moderate exercise are practical considerations worked out within group. Peer pressure and support work for women.

During a group using the checklist on Self-Destruction, as I reached the item on cutting, one of the women holding a baby had tears running down her cheeks. I asked, Was there a question? Something to share? "I cut my feet and then I walk on them." My question: " While you are using?" Her answer: "Since I was a child I have done this." My question: "Did your parents know? Did they do anything?" Her answer: "I would hide the cuts and walk on them for more pain. No one seemed to notice. My parents fought or drank most of the time." "Do you still cut your feet?" "When I don't have cocaine or alcohol." "You have three children; aren't you concerned they will notice?" "Yes, yes, I am here I thought for the cocaine found in my baby's system at birth. I now know I am here for my pain and destruction." A somber discussion by other group members with solid questions about the actual cutting as I caution: "Euphoric recall is not the goal." This was a difficult group to detach from. Everyone clearly learned something about the depths of despair cocaine and alcohol cause.

Overall the treatment goals are attained by slowly sorting out facts about abusive behaviors. Feelings of fear are clarified. Let us agree to disagree. Here again, I know I am preaching to the choir that sings recovery every working day. May you find some new ideas or a twist on old ideas to make your work rewarding. I am grateful to the 400 women in treatment over a 10-year period who bravely shared their pain and moved through it. They are my inspiration for this project. May you find yours. My gratitude to the many professionals writing about and working in this field without whose viewpoints I would not have seen this approach.

The 4A's Recipe

SETTING UP A GROUP

Recipe for Using the Posters and Handouts

All handouts, checklists, and written exercises included in this book can be copied and passed out to group members to reinforce material covered in the discussions.

In the back of the book are five posters needed at all sessions of this series. Tape the halves together, or order full-color versions using the form on page 75, and post them on the walls of the group's work space.

The importance of these posters is in their constant reminder of the issue:

FACTS V. FEELINGS.

Denial is, as we all know, that natural and normal defense mechanism gone out of control in addiction. My experience over time spent with clients becoming aware of abuse is their willingness to point out any of the items and discuss how it applies to them and to fellow group members. These posters keep the focus on what it is we are to be recognizing. Self-destruction without drugs or alcohol is subtle.

Recipe for Group

INGREDIENTS

1. Beginning and ending on time.
2. One person speaking at a time.
3. No abusive language = cussing, name calling, yelling.
4. Everybody shares — every opinion counts.
5. Agree to disagree even with the leader in an open honest tone (everyone taking turns).
6. Begin with 'I am an alcoholic/addict' name go-round (everyone taking turns).
7. End with an 'I am beautiful and I can . . .' affirmation.
8. Encourage journals of feelings after group.

PROCESS

I set my group time into three time frames, roughly held to by the day's activities. I go over each poster, giving examples and asking for feedback. I use the board and present as many examples as come to mind or come from the group. I sit down and open the discussion on one item; for example, "Hurt and let the work begin." I stir with questions. Any one of these questions will arouse interest:

1. Did you yell at anyone this morning? Hit someone?
2. Did someone yell at you? Hit you?
3. Was your mood dark? Feeling useless and unloved?
4. Were you anxious, nauseous, and uncomfortable about coming here?
5. Did a counselor forget to greet you / a group member?
6. Is there anyone in group that "makes" you feel intimidated?

IMPORTANT ELEMENT

I end every session with an **affirmation** — "I am" filled in individually by each group member. How many of you experienced group therapists are frustrated by this controlled process? I am a teacher. Presenting the material is my main goal. Like any teacher, involving the student in the process is important. Each of us has a personality and a set of tools. The important element here is the material. What we as professionals may take as sophisticated behavior, even normal behavior, our clients take as something they don't want or can't have. Letting the group know, you know this goes on, opens many doors.

Everyone in your group knows how to drink and drug, maybe not successfully, but repeatedly. They have no idea how they are behaving. Women using drugs and alcohol for rewards and/or for forgetting and/or for numbing need basic, childlike self-esteem building. The middle section where feedback and discussion occurs is when a co-leader or intern is needed for maximum gain. More than one skilled voice, one point of view, validates the information and the group. Today's funding says this is not a luxury; volunteers needing 12-step work or internship are available.

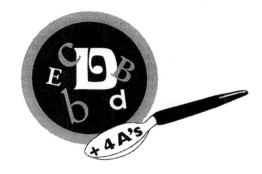

Basic Tools

DISCUSSIONS AND HANDOUTS

Recipe for Positive Change

HANDOUTS	*Affirmations* *10 Steps to Behavior Change*

BLEND

Affirmations used daily. Introduced in a process group giving many examples of positive attributes. Folders are handed out for the keeping of materials and the keeping of journals. As with any other exercise it may be used as a one-time addition to any group process, or incorporated into a structured program following the 4A = awareness, acceptance, action, attitude model.

STIR

It has been my experience and practice to repeat themes about recovery. I stress the need for abstinence and the tricks of the trade for not using any mind or mood altering chemicals. I believe and have seen the most successful recovering women become involved in a 12-step home group. Having people who don't use and a place where there are no drugs and things to do enhances the recovery process.

The most difficult A in the 4A's approach is the **attitude** about a whole life without chemicals. This is overwhelming to women, who have used something — sugar, caffeine, alcohol, cocaine, marijuana, sex — to calm themselves and make themselves more acceptable for many roles.

GOURMET

Goal of Group is to change our attitudes and outlooks and to become useful and happy sober human beings, able to fulfill all the roles in our lives with joy and maturity.

Affirmations

Remembering that affirmations are positive statements we want to believe about ourselves . . .

Let's take a moment to create those statements concerning all the roles we play in our lives . . .

Keep it simple and possible.

- ✪ First is the newest role as recovering addict: *sober, clean, clear, happy, calm.*
- ✪ Next is our role as a group member: *helpful, sober, honest, concerned.*
- ✪ Next is our role as a mother: *patient, understanding, firm, consistent, sober.*
- ✪ Next as a daughter: *mature, sober, loving, detached.*
- ✪ Next as a wife/girlfriend: *sober, clear, responsible, loving, kind, solid boundaries.*
- ✪ Next as a friend: *sober, available, loving, kind, independent.*
- ✪ Next as an employee: *timely, responsive, cooperative, sober.*
- ✪ Most important, as a human being: *sober, kind, happy, self-confident.*

HALT = hungry, angry, lonely, tired

turned into

nourished, honest, at a meeting, call a friend, take a nap.

Which are you willing to share? Which are you willing to give to a fellow group member? Which will you use today?

10 Steps to Behavior Change

1. Set a realistic goal for yourself — change one thing at a time!!

2. Be specific — "I will say my prayers every morning."

3. Please yourself — social pressure only works when people are around!!

4. Plan ahead — quitting smoking or adding prayer takes thought and preparation.

5. Ask for help — a burden shared is halved.

6. Try one positive and one negative together — add prayer and quit smoking!

7. Never say Never — people are human and stuff happens!!!

8. Use reminders — notes to yourself, string around finger, etc.

9. Keep a journal — record your progress and your feelings!!

10. Don't give up — Rome wasn't built in a day!!

THE most important behavior to change is to stop the use of alcohol and drugs!

Preparation

THE CHECKLISTS

Recipe for Denial Breaking: The Checklists

REMEMBER THAT EVERY JOURNEY BEGINS WITH A SINGLE STEP...

Stir daily for several days using the board and posters along with pencil, paper, and feedback.

MEASURE

I use these checklists as independent group exercises with pencil and paper, presentation, and discussion. The basic elements for breaking denial are here. Take what you like and leave the rest.

We professionals need to apply the basic tools with our own style. I mix the breaking of denial with the raising of self-esteem. Too much information without verbal hugs causes overload and loss of attention.

METHOD

I consider relapse a luxury for people with some clean time and success in recovery. Most group members merely lapse into old thinking and old patterns of friends and activities which bring on the **attitude** that only a drink or a drug can change.

Halfway through any series on self-destructive behaviors, it is important to remind the group of the real purpose for treatment: the removal of alcohol and drugs and the changing of everything. As professionals whatever side of the relapse debate we take, raising the **awareness** and **acceptance** of our clients is essential to quality treatment.

Self-Esteem

CHECK LIST

Before we 'hit' a drug, a child, a drink, ourselves:

____ I have said my mantra or prayer.

____ I have taken a long walk.

____ I have taken a bubble bath.

____ I have called a friend.

____ I have had a cup of tea.

____ I have listened to my favorite CD or TV show.

____ I have counted to 10 — twice.

____ I have counted my blessings.

____ I have thought about how bad it could be . . .

____ I hugged someone — even me . . .

____ I thought about my favorite 'safe' place.

____ I reminded myself of 'ODAT'.

____ I remembered 'this too shall pass'.

____ I looked at a picture of myself before recovery.

____ I remembered 'BLCS'.

ODAT = One Day At A Time
BLCS = Beautiful, Lovable, Capable, Sober

Parenting

CHECK LIST

Before we react to our child 'inside' or our children:

____ I take a 'time out'.

____ I admit powerlessness.

____ I identify my anger.

____ I choose an action: _____

____ I 'ignore' the other person, place, or thing.

____ I compliment my child.

____ I reward a positive behavior.

____ I set a new limit and a new consequence.

____ I model acceptable behavior.

____ I 'divert' the attention to a positive behavior.

____ I 'hug'.

____ I remind myself of the difference in our physical and mental sizes.

____ I remember who is the adult and how that feels.

____ I remember how it is to be a child.

____ I am _____

____ I am willing to change _____

**Time out formula = 1 minute x age of child
up to 10 minutes   15 minutes for adults**

Self-Destruction

CHECK LIST

Before we react to the 'inner beast' — let us make sure we are not harming ourselves:

_____ I took a drink or a drug.

_____ I skipped a meal or two.

_____ I stayed in isolation.

_____ I chewed my nails, scratched, or cut myself.

_____ I induced vomiting or used laxatives.

_____ I spent money I did not have.

_____ I had sex with someone for the 'fix.'

_____ I went to a bar in that 'old' place.

_____ I called my 'dealer.'

_____ I hit my child or spouse.

_____ I exercised for more than an hour.

_____ I decided not to bathe.

_____ I cut my hair and cut my hair.

_____ I stayed with someone who is still using.

_____ I spent time recalling past abuse.

_____ I let someone 'live rent free' in my head.

'Live rent free' *or* 'Keep the focus on me'

Self-Affirmation

CHECK LIST

Things I remind myself of daily:

_____ I am able to stay sober and clean today.

_____ I am beautiful, lovable, capable, sober.

_____ I hear my disease talking — I can say 'shut up.'

_____ I can change my feelings and attitudes.

_____ I am fundamentally 'good.'

_____ I deserve happiness.

_____ I trust myself.

_____ I deserve sober friends.

_____ I appreciate my program of treatment.

_____ I am powerless and I like it.

_____ I am able to love others and hate what they do.

_____ I am _____

_____ I deserve _____

_____ I appreciate _____

_____ I can _____

OCAT = One Change At A Time

23

Mixing, Stirring, Blending, and Folding

DISCUSSIONS AND HANDOUTS

Recipe for Attitude Adjustment

HANDOUTS

Attitude leads to the first drink.

INGREDIENTS: Paper and pencil or crayon exercise best done one point at a time in a group. Go around the table, take turns. We all have this attitude tone.

PACE (Positive Attitude Changes Everything)

STIR & BLEND

This discussion on a good day can lead to the following talk about PACE or to individuals sharing their tools for staying clean. My pattern is to stay as close to the primary sobriety goal as the group is willing. As we all know from our first experience in a group (remember kindergarten or play school), stating the goals and format are just guides for an emerging dynamic. Group is a challenging and rewarding experience.

Reinforce support beyond treatment. This is a good beginning for an introduction to Narcotics Anonymous — a little history of the fellowship being started in California where Alcoholics Anonymous members did not want to talk about drugs; this brought about a new textbook based on all the AA steps and traditions. Meetings are the same. The purpose is the same: to promote sober and clean living through a return to a higher power other than alcohol and drugs. In the meeting rooms it can be heard from one member to another "Keep the PACE."

There can be a lively discussion of recovery options and fears about these options. I sometimes find myself minimizing just how overwhelming it can be to change friends and activities. The familiar is not comfortable or healthy but the group knows how to be self-destructive and how to drink. It is important to take a few minutes here at the blackboard or have the group prepare a poster on what activities are available for fun where drugs and alcohol do not need to be. A positive attitude about nothing is nothing.

List or suggest the simple to complex. I find a poster and laughter work to alleviate the fear of boredom and change. Hobbies and entertainment can be sober activities.

Attitude leads to the first drink.

- Everyone is wrong about everything today!
- Nothing feels right!
- I do not need a meeting!
- Who really listens to their sponsor?
- Did you hear that?! What do they know?
- I can handle this!
- Bars are not a risky place!
- This job sucks!
- I'll never get ahead — who needs sobriety?
- I never drank that much!
- Cocaine is the in thing — nobody will know!
- Marijuana should be legalized anyway!
- .5% in non-alcoholic beer won't hurt!
- Who needs group?!!

PACE

Keep the PACE!

POSITIVE
ATTITUDE
CHANGES
EVERYTHING !!!!

✪

That looking at life as a half-full glass is better than a half-empty one.

✪

That counting blessings and keeping a gratitude list keeps the disease in its place.

✪

That people learn from what you do and not what you say.

✪

That action is better than self-pity.

✪

That every person has value and worth.

Recipe for Basic Alanon

INGREDIENT IS UNDERSTANDING

The most heartbreaking and difficult situations arise around the group's struggles with families' reactions to their new-found friends and attitudes. I reverse my order here in that I present the solution to the problem well before the problem.

The ideal situation is for the entire family to enter into recovery. My philosophy is to treat the person or persons in front of me. They may be willing to lose their fear of control over their loved ones if they understand what sending them to a support group or bringing them to a family activity will involve.

BOARD DISPLAY FOR BASIC ALANON TALK

- SSS = SIT DOWN! SHHHH! (shut-up) SMILE!
- CCC = CAUSE! CURE! CONTROL!
- CONTRIBUTE!!!!!
- GGG = GET OFF! GET OUT! GET ON!
- GOD = Good Orderly Direction

NECESSARY STEPS

STEPS 1-3: Practicing the three S's is the best way to avoid an argument. Early recovery is frustrating. Just not playing is the healthiest way to end the old. The new communication comes later. Modeling the results of not playing in the argument can be accomplished with role play using group members.

STEP 4: Understanding CCC. One of the facts of alcoholism is no one can make another person drink or drug. What adults drink or use in a free society is their responsibility. No matter how much yelling and blaming goes on, the **cause** of alcoholism is the drinker drinking. With all the research available there is still no **cure**; only abstinence will arrest the disease. The fact found most frustrating by everyone in early recovery is the inability to **control** others' behaviors and responses. Manipulation (playing puppet master) is a sickness. Direct communication is not successful until trust is established.

STEP 5: Admitting to the group your **contribution.** Yelling, blaming, avoiding, shaming, embarrassing, telling others, making excuses, lying are all part of the sickness that is the family disease of addiction.

STEPS 6-7: Get off their backs, **get out** of God's way and **get on** with your own life are the basic tenets of Alanon recovery.

Recipe for Basic Alanon

NECESSARY STEPS, CONT'D

STEPS 8-9: *Detachment with love* as we will discuss is what Alanon practices. Aids: staying clean and working a program! The treatment program is a role model for a new way of life without alcohol and drugs.

STEPS 10-12: For family members it is a life without worry and shame and guilt. I encourage family members to try abstinence. "Only people with a drinking problem can't or won't stop using."

BAKE AND COOL FOR 24 HOURS:

Both of these statements are loaded with the reality of life within an addicted family and are the lead-in to the next talk and handout on *Family Systems:*

- **Addiction is a family disease causing symptoms in the user and the "fixer" and the "scapegoat" and the others, too!**
- **Recovery is changing everyone and everything in the family system!**

Recipe for Understanding Dysfunction

HANDOUT	***Family System Disease Model*** Ingredients for understanding family dynamics.
METHOD	The group needs reassurance of the existence of these roles in others' lives. Part of the day's or days' exercises is always the time for feedback — a time to interact with the group on what you and they see as pretty usual behavior in an alcoholic environment. **Recovery also means restoration, getting back to normal (discussing what that is could be an entire group), quieting down, readjustment, improvement, reformation, heal, improve, regain, mend, GETTING WELL.** Synonyms for recovery are very effective words to use or display. I move back to the individual's recovery with *My Business*.
MEASURE	An overload of information can happen with the reality of these women's lives. The more sober the group becomes, the higher level of trust and the time limits will determine whether this can be successfully delivered in one to three sessions. Many families have recovered and stayed together while changing violent behavior. The group needs this affirmation. This may feel like **a hangover without the drugs** or it may feel like someone has run over you. Facts bring out feelings.

Family System Disease Model

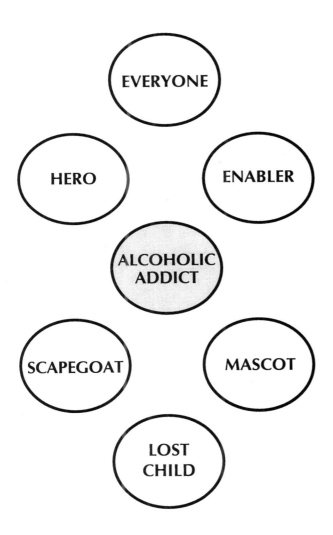

Enabler is the person who is invested in covering up the secret and protecting the family from shame. Mom or Dad or oldest child.

Hero is the person invested in letting the outside world know that everything is great because he/she is perfect! Every group has an overachiever. Every group member has a sibling who was the star. They are the best at everything. Hero children become overachieving adults who burn out early and come to treatment and can do well.

Mascot is interested in placating and minimizing the pain and abuse by cracking jokes and pleasing everyone! Humor/laughter is a healthy response to something funny, not a tool to avoid reality. Alcoholic families are filled with tension and mixed messages.

Scapegoat is interested in getting out and holding on — their role is to carry the pain of the secret and look worse than the "elephant." The Greek use for goats was to tie all the problems in a sack around the goat's neck and have them leave the village. How many people in the group are the family member who is the worst?

Lost Child is just lost, usually in fantasy and eating. Eating disorders are manifestations of unfulfilled nurturing. The lost child feels empty and alone. Food is a comfort. Denying food is a way to show the parent they don't need nurturing. Food addiction is a complex issue. Basic nutrition skills are essential to successful long-term recovery in all clients.

Everyone is what happens to most alcoholics and addicts — trying every method of coping until finally following the model of the addict.

Recipe for Understanding Dysfunction

HANDOUT

What Is My Business?

An exercise to further focus on sorting out just what is important in the **actions** and **attitudes** toward recovery.

METHOD

I recommend crayons for this exercise. What we are looking for is how complete the face is. Is a face all they draw? Is the body smaller than the face? Does anyone not have a picture? Are there clothes? Are there other people? Can you or anyone in the group find humor in their picture?

Is the group ready to face the facts about not knowing who they are or how they feel? Happy, Sad, Lonely, Glad, or Angry? I stick to the basics here. Cognitive awareness of the expansive number of words for feelings is not as important as recognizing feelings as existing without drugs.

Many women shut down and are awakened in a group with laughter and silliness. There have been days when this exercise brought tears. If an abuse victim trusts the group, revelations occur about their experience. This can help the group open up to the sadness and pain. Awareness of the existence of abuse is our goal. Accepting the unacceptable as happening to more than one of "us" is the beginning of healing.

What Is My Business?

Take a moment to think about what you are concerned about right now. Is it something or someone? Write a line or two explaining that concern.

OK! What can you do about this person, place, or thing? Just a line or two will do.

Now . . . Tell yourself what would be the perfect moment for you! A line or two!

Now . . . Tell yourself your three most favorite FUN activities. REMEMBER — no drugs or alcohol. A list is OK.

Now . . . Of all the things on this page — which could you accomplish for today?

Which would keep you sober today?

Finally . . . Turn this page over and draw a picture of yourself doing something that makes you feel OK! Everyone is doing this — it is not a contest or art lesson. We are going to talk about feelings!! Feelings, remember, are not right or wrong — they just are!!!!

Recipe for Recognizing Denial

HANDOUT	***Leveling* v. *Denial*** **Looking for all 4A's.** Really lively discussion can occur with a cooperative and motivated group.
INGREDIENTS	Handing out red crayons for circling what the group identifies with does several things: ✪ It keeps them focused; ✪ It raises the awareness of group commonality; ✪ It encourages lightness with the seriousness and internal responses I have no way of measuring.

Leveling *v.* Denial

Leveling is: openly owning our feeling!

Denial is:
Rationalizing, Justifying, Projecting, Blaming/Accusing, Judging/Moralizing, Intellectualizing, Analyzing, Explaining, Theorizing, Generalizing, Quibbling/Equivocating, Debating/Arguing, Sparring, Questioning/Interrogating, Switching, Denying, Being Smug/Superior/Arrogant, Minimizing, Evading/Dodging, Defiance, Attacking/Aggression, Withdrawing, Silence, Verbalizing/Talking, Shouting/Intimidating, Threatening, Frowning, Glaring, Staring, Joking, Grinning/Smiling/Laughing, Projecting, Agreeing, Complying

... wow!!!

Recipe for Basic Relationship Work

CODEPENDENCY = A PROGRESSIVE DISEASE OF THE BODY, MIND, AND SOUL

Codependency as Intimacy Dysfunction in primary relationships is a learned coping method. The physical and psychological implications for maintaining abstinence within one of these sick relationships are cunning and fascinating. Even when people are being abused they continue to cling to the idea of the relationship. An over-developed sense of loyalty with a progressive build-up is outlined here for the therapist's benefit.

HANDOUTS

I present this information in a conversational manner as preparation for the two handouts:

> *Me, Codependent?*
>
> *Feelings*

This is just another spin on the same disease. Removing alcohol and drugs has always seemed simpler to me than teaching the removal of unhealthy dependencies.

PROGRESSION OF THE DISEASE OF DEPENDENCE ON PEOPLE

EARLY STAGE: embarrassment; confusion; rationalization; fear; anxiety; apprehension; tension; false hopes; disappointment; guilt; isolation; alienation; euphoria; anger; disgust; protectiveness; genuine pity and sympathy; preoccupation with chemical dependency — **all feelings about the "other" person.**

MIDDLE STAGE: rejection; rage; panic; constant worry; concern for illness; personal frustration; lethargy/lack of motivation; hostile toward chemicals; hopelessness; punishes the abuser; self-pity; negative self; vindictive/bitch; distrust of self and others; rigidity; seriously uncommunicative; full dominance — chemical dependent has lost control, is out of center of family.

- **Shift occurs as anger and frustration increase and alcoholism becomes uncontrollable.**
- **The codependent has a personality change as dramatic as the active user, causing a ripple effect!**

CHRONIC STAGE: decline in independence; role reversal; withdrawal from other family and community members; fighting/nagging; verbal abuse; psychosomatic ailments; sexual problems; avoidance of social occasions where there is drinking; lying; covering up; threats; hiding; not being seen; paranoia about seeing others; more personal use of chemicals/joining in; self-absorbing isolation; no outlets; vacuum.

Recipe for Basic Relationship Work

PROGRESSION OF CODEPENDENCY, CONT'D

- Crisis brings one of the members to treatment or the doctor/hospital, or the courts or the support groups.
- Part of intervention is teaching the detachment game = sorting out who is responsible for what = chemical user for use and codependent for threats and nagging.

Women in treatment play both roles and find this information fuzzy. I focus on the chronic stage, where joining in the drug use to control and be involved with the partner lead to more violence and more chemical use. Recovery for one member of a using couple is a risky time. The user will be pulling on your client to join back in and play. I have seen many women leave treatment with and without black eyes in self-defense. Making a plan for leaving often takes more time than an impulsive addict or alcoholic is able to bear.

With the posters in the room at all times, I can stop and cover the cycle of violence and gently remind the women of the need for individual counseling and safety training. The basic element in safety training is to leave during the honeymoon stage. Having the shelter and hotline numbers available at all times is crucial. I have over the years had women call to say they did it — goodbye. One in 100 have the courage to give up their life and move to another town or state. A woman will leave an abusive situation on average five to seven times before or if she can finally stay away.

The goal here is to raise awareness and acceptance of the unacceptable and offer choices starting with abstinence. Two years may seem like a long time when we only have 12 to 18 weeks. My goal has been to offer the best information in the best environment possible.

Me, Codependent?

Discussion / Definition

Self-esteem   "I don't know what it feels like?"

Reality   "I make my own?"

Boundaries   "I have none that I recognize?"

Needs and Wants   "I don't know the difference?"

Moderation   "I don't know what it is?"

Shame   "I have it or guilt most all the time?"

Hostages   "I need them?"

Intimacy   "I am afraid of it?"

Behavior extreme   "I am either chaotic or controlling?"

Repression   "I need to hide my past — It's too painful?"

Suppression   "I don't remember — I won't remember?"

Disassociation   "I leave my body behind in the pain?"

Minimization   "I'm not that horrible — neither is anyone else?"

Delusion   " I'm not 'that kind of person' — neither is _____?"

Denial   "I did not did not have this happen to me?"

Our History   "I don't remember anything bad?"

Feelings   "I am frozen — no — out of control?"

Body language   "I don't understand what my body is saying?"

"I'm afraid, I'm ashamed, I'm angry, I'm worthless, I'm Co - Co - Codependent?"

Feelings

Just a few of the words — let us match them with experiences:

love   fear   warmth   worry   caring

sadness   patient   confused   violent

angry   victimized   frozen   out of control

in charge   right   wrong   hatred

ashamed   happy   shy   excited   guilty

angry   sympathy   moody   discouraged

encouraged   frustration   brave

courageous   sensitive   humorous   sad

glad   mad   gloomy   excited

pleased   hurt   embarrassed   jealous

understanding

ABUSED = HURT   ANGRY   CONFUSED

Written Exercise

Take a moment to describe and give an example of when/where, with whom?

POWERLESS =

USELESS =

HELPLESS =

Recipe for Awareness of Abuse

HANDOUT	***Awareness of Abuse*** Paper and pencil exercise followed by point by point sharing, "I Am" and fun.
SEASON & MIX 	This is an important point in domestic violence awareness. Women actively using do not feel they have the right of protest, or protest violently. These are the extremes of individual situations, again. Sharing them and identifying the middle road are important. Be careful. An abuser in the build-up stage of his or her cycle can be pushed to an act of violence if the change in the partner is too dramatic. This is a good time to remind the group about making a plan to leave/change. Something life-threatening needs time, care, and assistance to be safe. Safety is still the underlying and overtly spoken goal here. Hotline numbers repeated please.
METHOD	This material is a composite of experience and reading in the field of domestic violence and addictions. A high level of trust is necessary for maximum results. I have experienced many responses. Someone sees more clearly what is happening because of a combination of drug, alcohol, and emotional abuse. Women have left treatment and left their abusive relationships. Alanon talks about violence. Local hotlines have volunteers to answer questions about violence.
REMINDER	Follow up all groups with: The **"I Am"** game is a daily task that takes just a few minutes. **"I Am" beautiful, lovable, sober, capable, important, deserving.** Each person chooses the word that they are working on achieving for today. Every group can be followed by sadness; this sadness needs affirmation and diversion. Color crayons, arts and crafts, bring fun and fellowship.
COOL & SERVE	This material needs to be followed by intense work on **Detachment.** There are several ways to help the women with this emotional healing. In domestic violence physical removal is the last move. Statistically the victim will leave five times. This means there is work to do emotionally with the shame, guilt, blame, and of course the most obvious, but often missed, what next? Detachment is the full circle of the **4A's.** While working through the many exercises the group **becomes aware, accepts, takes action, and changes attitudes** on a daily basis. Long-term success is still in the hands of God. None of us has professionally found a way to take responsibility for the outcomes of our work after the client leaves our care. My best defense against the power of addiction is to do the best with each day and each group.

Awareness of Abuse

GUIDELINE: Anytime is a sign of trouble; there are no wrong or right answers; only looking for perceptions.

GOAL: What is it? Is it verbal abuse? Is it love?

RESPOND in writing and verbally with: yes, no, sometimes, most of the time, always, only when drinking or drugging.

- Does your partner seem irritated or angry at/with you several times a week?
- Does he/she deny being angry when he/she clearly is?
- Do your attempts to discuss feelings of pain or emotional distress result in a feeling that the issue has not been resolved? Not heard? Not understood?
- Do you frequently feel perplexed and frustrated by his/her responses, as though you were each speaking a different language? Not in the same space? On the same planet?
- Do you have a sense that you should not feel as bad/sad as you usually do?
- Is it fair to say your partner rarely (or never) seems to want to share thoughts or plans with you? Does it feel like "secrets" or "cheating" or "left out?"
- Thinking back, do you find that you can't recall ever saying "Cut it out!" or "Stop it!" to your partner? Are you afraid to set limits and boundaries?
- On issues of importance to you, does he/she typically respond with either anger or a claim that he/she has no idea what you are talking about? "Don't bother me."
- Are you able to say "Stop it" and be heard?
- Are you happy and content when you are with this person?
- Do you feel trapped?
- Are you in love or in hostage?
- Have you felt: exhausted, backache, headache, "stuffed in a box", "sick and tired", tense, confused, worthless, used up, stomach ache, itchy, sweaty, panicky?
- Does someone: tell jokes at your expense, trivialize, name call, order, discount, counter (change the subject, pass the blame), threaten, out-of-control anger?
- Close your eyes for a moment, breathe deeply, imagine life without this person. What do you see/feel/hope?

Recipe for Reference

HANDOUT

Vocabulary

METHOD: I use vocabulary handouts as introductions and repetition of ideas. Of course use these as a group exercise or two. I hope you have given out folders or notebooks for everyone to keep all this material in. I have gone ahead and made workbooks for the group, handed out three-ring binders when funding was available, bought the colored paper folders with pockets, given out large brown envelopes, left it to the group to organize. I am a go with the flow of the group therapist. Some groups function more efficiently than others, so being prepared is my job.

SEASONING

My favorite story after another didactic group presenting the same material in a different dress is about Pete and Repeat. They are two recovering men taking a walk by the river. They see two beautiful women on the other side. Pete jumps in. Who is left? Repeat! Sometimes I get a laugh — a groan — a comment, "Do we have to hear that again?"

Vocabulary

BOUNDARIES = Limits and guidelines set by parents for themselves and their children: bedtimes, meal times, language, chores, use of drugs, bathing, homework, family responsibilities, etc.

BOUNDARIES = limits set by adults for adult relationships both physical and emotional — where are you and where does the other person begin and end.

CHILD ABUSE = any time an adult's anger shows as a mark or scar on a child's body.

CHILD NEGLECT = any time a child's basic needs for food, shelter, love, medical care, education, and safety are not provided on a consistent basis.

DISCIPLINE = teaching the necessary skills and attitudes to live in society.

EMOTIONAL ABUSE = name-calling, criticism, role reversal, isolation, domination, lack of affection.

HALT = whenever you are Hungry, Angry, Lonely, or Tired — take care of yourself.

KISS = **Keep It Simple Sweetie** — stop and think.

NUTS = **Not Using The Steps,** stressing the importance of attendance at Alcoholics Anonymous or Narcotics Anonymous.

ODAT = **Living One Day At A Time,** remembering tackling one problem and staying in the moment will give a sober day.

PARENTING = loving, nurturing, protecting, and teaching.

PRIVILEGE = any activity or item given as a result of accomplishing a task = stickers, hugs, added responsibilities, literature, snacks.

RECOVERY = a combination of actions and attitudes used to change self-destructive behaviors. Sobriety is being free of chemicals and toxic thinking.

TASK = A responsibility shared and negotiated in a family for teaching and living.

TIME OUT = Parenting tool using one minute for each year of age for the child and parent to cool-off. Example: five minutes for a five-year-old (1x5=5). Early recovery gives addicts and alcoholics the attention span of five year olds.

Vocabulary

TIME OUT PLACE = A chair or pillow or room where the child can think and wait. This works for adults in early recovery.

SELF ABUSE = Using alcohol, drugs, cutting, starving, bingeing, purging, spending, acting out sexually, 'hanging out' in dangerous places with dangerous people, not sleeping, using sleep to escape, eating to escape, criticizing self, missing treatment, missing meetings, etc.

SEXUAL ABUSE = Physical and mental experiences against the will and/or knowledge of a minor. Rape is the term for adult sexual abuse.

RECOVERY PROGRAM = Usually a group actively involved in educating and changing addictive behaviors. Choices.

ADDICTIVE BEHAVIORS = Loss of control of the use of a substance or action that leads to negative consequences. Hitting a loved one, going to bars, getting too hungry, angry, lonely, tired are addictive behaviors.

AWARENESS = The first step in solving a problem is recognizing and owning it.

ACTION = Any new behavior taken to end an addictive behavior.

ACCEPTANCE = The ability to look at life on life's terms.

ATTITUDE = is the glass half full or half empty? Am I a valuable human being worth loving?

Baking and Cooling

GROUP EXERCISES

Aftercare Planning

GOD in our lives for today is **Good Orderly Direction!**

Three responsibilities for continued sobriety are:

1. Attend an AA (Alcoholics Anonymous) meeting and purchase a copy of *Living Sober* (yellow, 87 pages). This is your text for living for the next year.

2. Practice **HALT** daily. When you are **hungry** eat something healthy. When you are **angry** talk to someone about it. When you are **lonely** go to a meeting or call a 'new' friend.

3. Participate in your group even when you don't want to. Talk about the good, the bad, and the ugly. Ask questions, give feedback, complain, cry, and laugh.

HOW — by being as **honest** as you can, being **open-minded** about treatment and recovery, being **willing** to try new thoughts and behaviors.

How long is **ODAT – One Day at a Time.**

EXERCISE

Above, and on the next two pages, we have a combined didactic presentation on aftercare planning (with a reminder of why we are planning aftercare), with first-step work and take-home work carried over into an afternoon of play on detachment.

Aftercare Planning

FIRST STEP INVENTORY

Write these PPT down as they come to mind. If you need more space to write that shows progress in honesty.

People who impacted your drinking and drugging:

Places where you drank and drugged:

Things you drank and drugged at:

RECOVERY INVENTORY

If you need more space to write — great. If not — great; quality over quantity.

People who make recovery possible:

Places where recovery is possible:

Things good for recovery:

Aftercare Planning

FIRST STEP QUESTIONS

1. Times you got drunk or high when you did not plan it:

2. Times family asked you to leave – threw you out:

3. Times you lied or cheated for drugs or a drink:

4. Most dollars spent on alcohol and/or drugs in one binge:
    a. Did you have that money?
    b. Did you spend grocery money?
    c. Did you steal the money — beg for it — do something you normally would not if sober?

5. Times you have been arrested — stopped by the police — done something illegal — caught or not:

6. Times you took the pledge and did not make it:

7. Times you said you had the flu when you were really hung-over and other excuses:

8. Your story with alcohol and drugs:

9. Your hopes for life without your addiction:

10. Your plan — one thing at a time — take your time:
    a. Sponsor:
    b. Home group:
    c. Telephone book of new sobriety contacts:
    d. Meeting schedule:
       Other:

Recipe for Detachment

DETACHMENT = REMOVING THE EMOTIONS FROM THE FACTS

Detachment is an idea that bears repeating. Now is a time to repeat **Basic Alanon** and to remove some of the barriers pencil and paper give. Women become addicted to alcohol and drugs often after being addicted to a mate or parent or child. Emotional clarity and empowerment are gained by repeated exercises in detachment.

INGREDIENTS

An increased involvement in **physical action** has proved effective for me. **Laughter** occurs when women struggle with these hoops and drawings. A keen and clear message of the emotional struggle in relationships is modeled here as an individual struggle. A reinforcement of the inability to change anyone but oneself is reinforced with humor.

EXERCISE

Uses Hula Hoops or chalk circles on the floor. Idea here is to discuss separate yet together concepts in major relationships. Often alcohol or drugs can be used as the relationship, especially if clients are not yet six weeks clean. As the diagram suggests, overlap the circles and ask the client to raise one Hula Hoop without disturbing the other. Then set the Hula Hoops side by side and ask the same thing. Discuss the ease with which circles (people) side by side can move versus those that are overlapped and not clear about who is on top. The chalk circles can be moved in the mind. Hula Hoops are more fun.

When the client is in a singular circle, ask them to share with the group three things about themselves that make them who they are. Keep a running list on the board of characteristics that group members share (strong, independent, safe, uncomfortable).

When the client is in the overlapping circles ask them to give three things about themselves. Keep a separate list on the board of overlapping characteristics (awkward, confined, silly, frustrated).

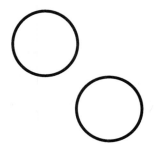

Using the two lists and the responses to lifting the circles, lead a discussion on and validate individual strengths of character. If the group is mature enough, compare those strengths shared with other group members and those weaknesses shared in the overlapping situation.

Goal is to look at the problem in a concrete way and begin to feel identification with others with the same dependencies. Be careful in using the word "dependent." There is a great deal of false pride that could disrupt the real goal of the exercise. The women feel foolish at first playing with Hula Hoops. Playfulness is affirmed as a positive characteristic for sustaining recovery and for being a contributing group member.

More Detachment

METHOD

Detachment is an idea that provides emotional relief for women addicted to others and others' approval. To present this idea there are several techniques used over several sessions. Below is a session for women with some background and awareness of their problem with a person, place, or idea.

EXERCISE

The set-up for this is as a playful time for the child within. The supplies are crayons, glitter, drawing paper, stickers, paste, glue, buttons, art supplies for the child within. A table is helpful, but not necessary. This works best as a group activity for feedback. I use this exercise after lunch and after a morning session of Good Orderly Direction. There are a great many decisions to make, and play can release tension and open discussion at the same time.

There are specific things to look for in play. This is not art — this is fun and this is detachment through awareness. Use the basics for setting, reassuring the clients of the awareness goal and the no-art class/play tone. Present this project simply and directly. Do not complicate the instructions or the time. Discussion after is the time for group involvement.

The idea of the project is to show the client surrounded by everything they love and loves them. Give a little extra time here for creativity and comfort. Some examples leave vague as to people, places, things. We want the thoughts of positive influences to be emphasized. The ideas about home groups and sponsors are still in the air from the morning.

As the therapist conducting the exercise, I share my own work. It helps to point out the subtle differences in size of figures and positioning on the paper. In particular I am looking for a change in position, with the client's life and loves becoming larger than the abuser/drugs.

I have observed wonder and laughter and bonding occurring within group when the sequins and glue become play. There is always that group unable to relax and play. It never stopped me trying this. I offer treats and throw in nutrition information found on the box of cereal or crackers, and of course on unhealthy, but fun sodas.

More Detachment

CRAFTS EXERCISE, CONT'D.

Things to look for in picture to assess openness and honesty; numbers and types of items (people, places, things, ideas).

Colors and varieties and overall enthusiasm for play are important markers of a return of feelings.

GOURMET

Goal of this exercise is to share feelings of relief and empowerment over one's self, allowing self-esteem to grow from the inside little child outward. The awareness of how giving personal power to drugs is emotionally limiting and addicting are also discussed. Going from 'problem' to 'solution' with ease in the whole exercise is important.

Be willing to carry the discussion into affirmation cards and to give the pictures with affirmation cards as gifts from the client to themselves. (Affirmation cards are 3x5 pocket cards of the day's "I Am" ending.) Putting the pictures on group room bulletin board to share and be proud of where setting allows is also very useful.

Recipe for Self-Esteem

INGREDIENTS

This is an exercise in values best used toward the end of treatment. I have enjoyed this exercise in mixed groups as well as women's groups. It is interesting to see the struggle for some to give up stereos and others children and many partners. In the end survival/sobriety is the lesson. Even if you have lost everything, sobriety has as much value as life.

Handled carefully this can be a playful and meaningful time for the group. They know each other and are comforted by their differences and similarities. Group leadership emerges as the choices become more difficult. The most successful processing of this group takes place sitting on a circle on the floor. Comfort is gone before we start.

MEASURE

This is an exercise in values and making choices. The goal is to facilitate conversation that will explore how and why we prioritize choices. The object is to begin the process of looking at life as a whole without the drugs and/or alcohol.

BLEND

We begin by presenting the goals and objects and stating the rules:
1. Everyone may bring four things with you on this cruise; they may be people, places, or things.
2. Everyone may NOT bring drugs or alcohol. Every necessity is provided by the cruise staff.

EXERCISE

Draw a ship on the board including the levels shown below, making sure that Higher Power is on the top and recovery tools are in the middle.

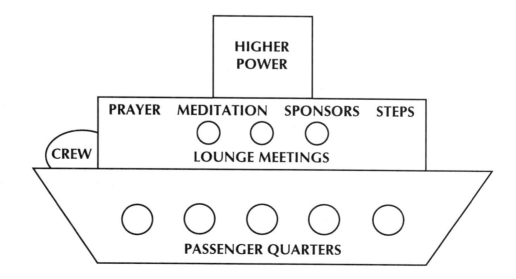

Recipe for Self-Esteem

CRUISE SHIP EXERCISE, CONT'D

SUGGESTIONS

Use the space below the ship to list the names and the items each person has chosen. Then begin the journey in a peaceful, recovery-oriented mood. After everyone becomes restless introduce the idea of an approaching storm and ask that each passenger give up one item to lighten the ship and protect against the storm. Make comments on struggles with the choices.

Now move the level of fear to include water coming on board. Ask each person to choose two items to throw overboard to save their lives. Look for drama and levity. Discuss each person's choices with humor and understanding. The final choice on this cruise will be between the passenger and their final item.

Now is the time to point out how things and other people have value in comparison to themselves and their recovery. Self has a place in recovery. Allow time for everyone to give and receive feedback.

BAKE, COOL & SERVE

End the session with an affirmation of personally stated value: "I am the most important part of my recovery" and an assignment to journal any after-exercise feelings and responses. This is a good session to serve snacks and have a going away party or a sobriety chip award or any program recognition ceremony.

Serving

AFTERWORDS

Closing Statement

I hope these exercises have given you familiar and new ingredients in our continued struggle with this insidious disease. This text completes the circle I started with a Master's thesis on "Parenting and Preventing Child Abuse" and a Ph.D. thesis on "Preventing Self Abuse and Self Destruction in Addicted Women."

I work in the moment. I have basic guidelines for what I wish to present and for measuring the results of the presentations and discussions. I have worked with several different groups of women rotating through treatment. Each combination of individuals responded as a group with mixed emotions to the realities I present. I measured the day only.

My experiences have taught me to respect alcohol and drugs as powerful destroyers of people. I look at our job as catalysts for the explosion of recovery. We work. We just don't see results immediately. Two years is the time we all agree on for the physical, emotional, and economic recovery from active abuse of drugs.

May you find these materials useful in your daily work. I personally keep a computer file for turning clients over to a higher power. I call it my God File. None of us works alone against this baffling illness. None of us is more powerful than alcohol. May you find peace.

Basic Recipe for Recovery

Ingredients: found in all our group members, mixed with all our professional skills and raised with the yeast of patience and time.

Denial by the pound

Information by the ton

Treatment by the day

Sponsorship when ready

Confrontation when needed

Validation daily

Affirmation daily

Stirred liberally with new friends found at 12-step groups

Baked slowly in an atmosphere warm with fun activities.

Results are disease *awareness accepted* with an *attitude* filled with the *actions* of people back into life on life's terms.

Food for Thought

PEBBLES AND POPCORN

The idea came to me as I sat listening to a friend share her pain about her life. Martyrdom is a choice made by many of us who find suffering a way of life. The idea of Christ being stoned as the ultimate sacrifice frustrates many of us. We think our petty grievances deserve stoning when being pelted with pebbles is an exaggeration. Popcorn is more like the actual experience.

Growing up with active alcoholism and its "no safety net," brings many responses. The one in direct opposition to martyrdom is the critic who relentlessly puts the sufferer down with reminders of how lucky we are to be a part of life. There is some truth; living for the sake of living is the goal of a God-directed life. Active alcoholism "should" only hurt the drinker. Problem is that is not true. Many people struggle in Alanon for a reasonable answer to an unreasonable situation. It is living on quicksand. There is a slow steady descent into nothingness while the drinker drinks and forgets to notice what is going on around him or her.

The other phenomenon is the "driver of the bus," as the only person who knows where everyone is going. The chief enabler navigates this unknown destination with hope of controlling the uncontrollable. Everyone else exists to fit the agendas of the enabler and alcoholic. I did not cause this disease, I can not cure it, and I most certainly can not control the disease nor the person caught in the disease. I must live my own life to good purpose from today forward. It feels like boulders while trying to control the uncontrollable. It feels like popcorn when I detach.

— *Anonymous*

The Cookbook

RESOURCES

Recipe for Counselor's Understanding

INGREDIENTS, HERBS & SPICES OF ADDICTION

Intimacy Dysfunction: developmental or pathological barrier to engaging in intimate behavior. Symptoms: physical abuse, emotional neglect, sexual abuse of children, relationship discord, violent relationships, rape, sexual dysfunction with chemical dependency. *Boundary setting is essential to recovery process.*

Chemical Abuse: use for "normal" functioning; dependence to produce positive feelings, to feel relaxed; inability to "control" use; loss of control/socially accepted behavior.

Chemical Dependency: use with harmful consequences; preoccupation with use; loss of control of amounts or frequency; alcohol and/or drugs; physical and/or psychological dependence.

Codependency: covert or overt learned pattern of exaggerated dependency with identity confusion with painful consequences.

Intimacy: in a relationship it is the ability to express positive and negative feelings in a constructive way — intellectual or social or sexual or spiritual.

Sexual Activity: one form of intimacy.

Sexuality: includes physical, gender, sex-role, and sexual orientation identity with needs for warmth, tenderness, touch, love. *Emphasis on learning to feel without chemicals.*

Child Abuse: visible physical harm.

Child Neglect: not providing food, shelter, education, medical care, and emotional needs for safety. Emphasis on drunkenness as neglect.

Marital-Relationship Problems: breakdown of appropriate roles; sexual identity conflicts; poor communication skills; unhealthy attitudes and values about intimacy and sex; violence. *Emphasis all early recovery married clients.*

Family Conflict: comes before, after, during active use of alcohol and drugs.

Addictive Disorders: gambling, sex, spending, binge/purge eating, dieting, exercising connect to chemical abuse. Any number of clients with more than one active addiction — any number of recovering people with the emergence of "other" addictions.

Family Dynamics: those boundary and intimacy attitudes that surface in addicted individuals as a result of childhood experiences.

Shame: a feeling of unworthiness or sinfulness or unwanted — excuses for and result of chemical abuse.

Boundary Inadequacy: ambiguous, overly rigid, or invasion of physical or psychological space. *Recovery requires boundary setting work.*

Perpetrators of Incest: lacks skills in boundary setting and respecting others' boundaries, experiences early childhood sexual trauma, alcohol abuse, family dysfunction at core. *Women alcoholics (75 percent) victims.*

INGREDIENTS, HERBS & SPICES OF ADDICTION

Pedophiles: child molester, 52 percent alcoholic; both problems need treatment attention.

Rapists: crime of violence with a 50 percent alcohol use at arrest and 35 percent MAST result. Prescott theory of not enough physical pleasure in the formative years is significant to chemical dependency as a substitute for pleasure as well.

Violence: symptom of intimacy dysfunction involving chemical abuse, not caused by chemical abuse. Carder reports 72 percent of wives of alcoholics in survey reported physically threatened, 45 percent beaten, 27 percent potential for admitting abuse. An issue in treatment that deserves consideration as a separate concern — *removing chemicals does not remove violence.* Family history of violence is also present. *As learned a response as drinking.*

Confusion of Roles: who is the mother, companion, marriage partner/child, husband. Children act like adults and replace their alcoholic parent to keep the family together.

Communication Difficulties: defensiveness, self-centeredness, dishonesty, blaming, withdrawal, resentment, desire to punish, boundary invasion. Aftercare and Alanon important to recovering couples.

Intimacy and Sexual Attitudes and Values: review of negative attitudes found in chemical abuse, shame-based value systems. Need teaching of openness and honesty.

Sexual Dysfunction: affects success of recovery — caused by chemical abuse and chemical influence on social history. Treatment needs run from simple education to specialized sex therapy. Men and women have impotency problems without and because of alcohol and drugs.

Shame: important in understanding addiction, co-dependency, sexual abuse, intimacy dysfunctions, and sexual difficulties.

Intervention on Shame: emphasis on connecting emotions, behaviors, and beliefs.

Boundary Inadequacy: pattern of ambiguous, overly rigid, or invasive to physical or psychological space — correlated to chemical dependency in individuals and families. Counter transference issues need attention.

Dependence and Caring: need clarifying when teaching boundaries.

Enmeshment: families allow little to no outside involvement. Individuation and separation fought by parents. Crisis-oriented behavior. Emphasis on education and support groups for all members.

Identity Disorder: internal and external points of reference distorted. Shame is key. Education and exposures to 'healthy' models.

Identity Reformation: individual work necessary to recovery.

COUNSELOR'S THOUGHTS

Looking for insights into the importance of individuation, education, ending isolation, and treating shame as a key treatment issue. Awareness of the physical effects of drugs on intimacy dysfunction is heightened.

What — all of this is out of control! Where do we start? Can we finish?

Bibliography

Alcoholics Anonymous. *Alcoholics Anonymous* (Third Edition). AA World Services, New York, 1976.

Al-Anon. *Al-Anon Faces Alcoholism* (2nd Edition). Al-Anon Family Group Headquarters, New York, 1984.

Bass, Ellen and Laura Davis. *Beginning to Heal.* Harper Perennial, Boston, 1993.

Black, Claudia. *Double Duty.* Ballantine Books, New York, 1990.

Coleman, Eli. *Chemical Dependency and Intimacy Dysfunction.* The Haworth Press, Binghamton, New York, 1988.

Condron, Daniel R. *Permanent Healing.* SOM Publishing, Windyville, Missouri, 1992.

Davies, Jody Messler & Mary Gail Frawley. *Treating the Adult Survivor of Childhood Sexual Abuse.* Basic Books, New York, 1994.

Davis, Martha, Elizabett Eshelman, Matthew Mckay. *The Relaxation & Stress Reduction Workbook.* New Harbinger Publications, Inc., 1988.

Drews, Toby Rice. *Getting Them Sober.* Recovery Communications, Inc., Baltimore, Maryland, 1990.

Edmonson, Karen. *Dual and Multiple Addictions — Treatment Manual.* American Continuing Education, Inc. 1994.

Fleming, Martin. *101 Support Group Activities.* Johnson Institute-Qvs, Inc., Minneapolis, Minnesota, 1992.

Gray, John. *Men Are From Mars, Women Are from Venus.* Harper Collins Publishers, New York, 1992.

Foely, Dennis & Eileen Nechas. *Women's Encyclopedia of Health & Emotional Healing.* Rodale Press, Inc., Emmaus, Pennsylvania, 1993.

Halpern, Howard M. *Cutting Loose.* Simon and Schuster, New York, 1976.

John, Roger & Peter McWilliams. *You Can't Afford the Luxury of a Negative Thought.* Prelude Press, Los Angeles, California, 1988.

Kroll, Jerome. *PTSD/borderlines in Therapy.* W.W. Norton & Company, Inc., New York, 1993.

Larsen, Ernie. *Old Patterns, New Truths: Beyond the Adult Child Syndrome.* A Harper/Hazelden Book, Minnesota, 1988.

Lerner, Harriet Goldhor. *The Dance of Deception.* Harper Collins, New York, 1993.

Mahoney, Michael J. *Self-Change Strategies For Solving Personal Problems.* W.W. Norton & Company, New York, 1979.

Marlin, Emily. *Relationships in Recovery.* The Philip Lief Group, Inc., New York, 1990.

May, Gerald G. *Addiction & Grace.* HarperCollins Publishers, New York, 1988.

Mellody, Pia. *Facing Codependence.* Harper and Row, San Francisco, 1989.

Miller, Dusty. *Women Who Hurt Themselves.* Basic Books, A Division of Harper Collins Publishers, New York, 1994.

BIBLIOGRAPHY

Minuchi, Salvador and H. Charles Fishman. *Family Therapy Techniques.* Harvard University Press, Boston, 1981.

Mycek, Shari. "Cries and Whispers." *Trustee Magazine,* Medford, New Jersey, May 1996.

Narcotics Anonymous. *Narcotics Anonymous.* NA World Services, California, 1988.

Northrup, Christiane, M.D. *Women's Bodies, Women's Wisdom.* Bantam Books, New York, 1994.

Peck, Scott M. *The Different Drum: Community Making and Peace.* Simon and Schuster, New York 1987.

Peurifoy, Reneau Z. *Anxiety, Phobias, & Panic.* Warner Books, Inc., New York, 1995.

Potter-Efron, Ronald & Patricia. *The Treatment of Shame and Guilt in Alcoholism Counseling.* The Haworth Press, New York, 1988.

Potter-Efron, Ronald & Patricia. *Aggression, Family Violence and Chemical Dependency.* The Haworth Press, New York, 1990.

Rogers, Ronald R. and C. Scott McMillan, Morris A. Hill. *The Twelve Steps Revisited.* Education & Training Institute of Maryland, Inc., 1985.

Sampson, Edward E. and Mary Marthas. *Group Process for the Health Professions.* John Wiley & Sons, Inc., New York, 1981.

Selby, Daniel R. with Manfred von Luhmann, M.D. *Conscious Healing.* Bantam Books, New York, 1991.

Stein, Diane. *The Natural Remedy Book for Women.* The Crossing Press, 1992.

Taubman, Stan. *Ending the Struggle Against Yourself.* G.P. Putman's Sons, New York, 1994.

Wachtel, Ellen F. *Treating Troubled Children and Their Families.* The Guilford Press, New York, 1994.

Waites, Elizabeth A. *Trauma and Survival.* W.W. Norton & Co., Inc., New York, 1993.

Wegsheider, Sharon. *Another Chance: Hope and Health for the Alcoholic Family.* Science and Behavior Books, Inc., California, 1981.

Internet Resources

The National Clearinghouse for Alcohol and Drug Information at:
http://www.health.org

The National Association for Children of Alcoholics at:
www.health.org/nacoa/

The Recovery Network at **http://recovery.netwiz.net/**

Comprehensive Guide for resources at:
http://www.hopeandhealing.com/aguide.htm.

A recovery home page at: **http://www.hubplace.com/addictions**

The World Health Organization at: **http://www.who.ch/**

The Rational Recovery Systems at: **http://www.rational.org/recovery**

Hazelden literature and treatment at: **http://hazelden.org**

A home page for treatment facilities at: **http://hubplace.com/addictions**

Amazon books web site for Addictions at:
http://www.optilube.com/recovery.htm

The National Institute of Health at: **http://www.nida.nih.gov/**

Alanon at: **http://www.alanon-alateen.org**

Alcoholics Anonymous at: **http://www.alcoholics-anonymous.org/**

World Wide Meeting Directory at: **http://www.aa-intergroup.org**

Resources for Professionals at: **http://www.lapage.com/art/**

Power and Control Wheel

Outer ring: **PHYSICAL VIOLENCE • SEXUAL VIOLENCE**

Center: **POWER AND CONTROL**

USING COERCION AND THREATS
Making and/or carrying out threats to do something to hurt her • threatening to leave her, to commit suicide, to report her to welfare • making her drop charges • making her do illegal things.

USING INTIMIDATION
Making her afraid by using looks, actions, gestures • smashing things • destroying her property • abusing pets • displaying weapons.

USING EMOTIONAL ABUSE
Putting her down • making her feel bad about herself • calling her names • making her think she's crazy • playing mind games • humiliating her • making her feel guilty.

USING ISOLATION
Controlling what she does, who she sees and talks to, what she reads, where she goes • limiting her outside involvement • using jealousy to justify actions.

MINIMIZING, DENYING AND BLAMING
Making light of the abuse and not taking her concerns about it seriously • saying the abuse didn't happen • shifting responsibility for abusive behavior • saying she caused it.

USING CHILDREN
Making her feel guilty about the children • using the children to relay messages • using visitation to harass her • threatening to take the children away.

USING MALE PRIVILEGE
Treating her like a servant • making all the big decisions • acting like the "master of the castle" • being the one to define men's and women's roles.

USING ECONOMIC ABUSE
Preventing her from getting or keeping a job • making her ask for money • giving her an allowance • taking her money • not letting her know about or have access to family income.

Courtesy of:
THE Domestic Abuse Intervention Project
202 East Superior Street
Duluth, Minnesota 55802
218-722-2781
Also available in poster size.

NONVIOLENCE

Equality Wheel

NEGOTIATION AND FAIRNESS
Seeking mutually satisfying resolutions to conflict • accepting change • being willing to compromise.

NON-THREATENING BEHAVIOR
Talking and acting so that she feels safe and comfortable expressing herself and doing things.

RESPECT
Listening to her non-judgmentally • being emotionally affirming and understanding • valuing opinions.

TRUST AND SUPPORT
Supporting her goals in life • respecting her right to her own feelings, friends, activities and opinions.

HONESTY AND ACCOUNTABILITY
Accepting responsibility for self • acknowledging past use of violence • admitting being wrong • communicating openly and truthfully.

RESPONSIBLE PARENTING
Sharing parental responsibilities • being a positive non-violent role model for the children.

SHARED RESPONSIBILITY
Mutually agreeing on a fair distribution of work • making family decisions together.

ECONOMIC PARTNERSHIP
Making money decisions together • making sure both partners benefit from financial arrangements.

EQUALITY

Courtesy of:
THE DOMESTIC ABUSE INTERVENTION PROJECT
202 East Superior Street
Duluth, Minnesota 55802
218-722-2781
Also available in poster size.

The Posters

TO USE THE BLACK AND WHITE POSTERS:

Tape together using page 9 as a guideline.

TO ORDER POSTERS IN FULL COLOR:

Color versions of these 11" x 17" posters are available for **$20.00 per set**.
Laminated color versions are available for **$30.00 per set**.

SHIP POSTERS TO:

Name: _____

Street: _____

City: _____ State: _____ Zip: _____

Phone: _____ Fax: _____

E-Mail: _____

	# OF SETS	PRICE
Plain Set(s)		
Laminated Set(s)		
	SHIPPING AND HANDLING	$4.50
	TOTAL	

Mail this form with check or money order made out to:
Belle Vista Graphics
3802 Parkmont Avenue
Baltimore, Maryland 21206-2420
Phone/Fax: 410-254-0804 • E-mail: bvgraph@aol.com

Hurt? ANGRY? Confused?

OUT OF CONTROL?

**What are the facts?
Do they match
the feelings?**

CYCLE OF VIOLENCE

Honeymoon ➜ Verbal Abuse ➜ Physical Act

TIME FOR BOTH:

1 Day to 1 Year.

Average Is 6 Months.

RELATIONSHIP DEVELOPMENT STAGES

Meet ➜ Get Acquainted ➜ Date with Friends ➜ Become Companions ➜ Flirt ➜ Discuss Sexual Relationship and Commitment!!

ADDICTION IS INSTANT!

RED FLAGS

- It has never been this good!
- I am losing control!
- We do not need anyone or anything else!
- Drug and/or chemical abuse!
- Unpredictable personality change!
- Confused! Angry! Sad!

Elements of a HEALTHY RELATIONSHIP

- **COMMUNICATION**
- **UNDERSTANDING**
- **BEING CONCERNED**

Mixed generously with separate yet shared programs of recovery

- **TRUST**
- **MUTUALITY**
- **SHARING**
- **RESPECT**
- **FRIENDSHIP**
- **ATTRACTION**

PARENTING

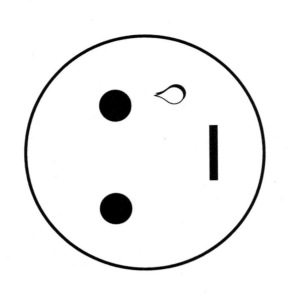

=

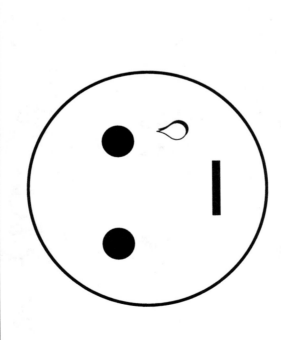

Hurt equals Hurt EXCEPT to someone who has been or is being abused. *THEN:*

Hurt equals much needed Attention.

Hurt equals Hitting.
Hurt equals Words.
Hurt equals Love.

choices → ADDICTION

- Drinking more often/more of
- Doing and saying embarrassing things
- Going places with dangerous people
- Family upset
- Legal problems
- Family separation
- Medical problems
- Job problems
- Lost cars
- More money problems
- Rage and violence toward self and others
- Social isolation
- Agitation and irritation
- Hospitalization
- Jail
- Death

RECOVERY

- Craving gone
- Apologizing and being accepted
- Going to work
- Family meetings and activities
- Seek employment/pay fines
- Family attends Al-Anon
- Mind begins to clear
- Attend AA/NA meetings
- Recognize out of control life
- Eat/sleep/exercise
- Treat anger
- New friends and activities
- Seek sponsorship
- Ask for medical advice
- Stop drinking
- Seek help

TIME FOR SERIOUS CHANGE!